HAL LEONARD
STUDENT
PIANO
LIBRARY

Piano Ensembles

Four-part student ensembles with conductor's score and optional accompaniment

LEVEL ONE 1

Arranged by Phillip Keveren

Featuring four student favorites from
Piano Lessons Book 1 of the *Hal Leonard Student Piano Library*

TABLE OF CONTENTS

Hal Leonard Student Piano Library Authors
Barbara Kreader • Fred Kern • Phillip Keveren • Mona Rejino

Piano Ensembles Level 1 is designed for use with the first book of most piano methods. Some methods may label their first book as *Book 1* (such as the *Hal Leonard Student Piano Library*), and others may label their first book a *Primer*.

Concepts in *Piano Ensembles Level 1*:

Range	Symbols	Keyboard Guides
	p, f, mp, mf	show hand placement
Rhythm 4/4 time signature	Intervals steps and skips only	L.H. / R.H. F G A B C D E 4 3 2 1 1 2 3

ISBN 978-0-7935-9214-2

HAL•LEONARD®

Visit Hal Leonard Online at
www.halleonard.com

World headquarters, contact:
Hal Leonard
7777 West Bluemound Road
Milwaukee, WI 53213
Email: info@halleonard.com

In Europe, contact:
Hal Leonard Europe Limited
1 Red Place
London, W1K 6PL
Email: info@halleonardeurope.com

In Australia, contact:
Hal Leonard Australia Pty. Ltd.
4 Lentara Court
Cheltenham, Victoria, 3192 Australia
Email: info@halleonard.com.au

FOREWORD

Piano study doesn't need to be lonely any more! These ensemble versions of favorite piano pieces from the *Hal Leonard Student Piano Library* will give students the pleasure and inspiration of playing with their friends.

Each selection includes:
- A conductor's score with optional teacher accompaniment

- Four student parts:
  Parts I and II for the first piano
  Parts III and IV for the second piano

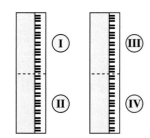

Four players at two pianos will be able to give a full and appropriate performance of each piece, yet more combinations of players and instruments are possible.

Here are some ideas:
- Use four digital pianos or electronic keyboards that allow students to play the suggested instrumentation for each part.

- Double, triple, or quadruple the student parts.*

- Add the optional teacher accompaniment, designed for both rehearsal and performance, by using an additional piano or keyboard.

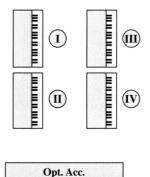

If students are using a keyboard that lacks a suggested sound, other voices may be substituted. For example, if an instrument does not have "Glockenspiel," use any available similar sound, such as "Vibes" or "Marimba." If "Oboe" is unavailable, use any similar sustaining sound, such as "Flute," "Clarinet," or "Strings."

We hope you and your students will enjoy the challenges and pleasures of playing these exciting ensembles. Strike up the piano band!

Barbara Kreader   Fred Kern   Phillip Keveren   Mona Rejino

Night Shadows

Conductor's Score & Optional Accompaniment

Performance Configurations

Two Pianos

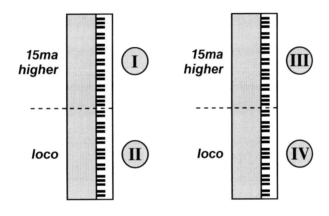

OR

Four Keyboards
(with suggested instrumentation)

Night Shadows

Barbara Kreader
Arranged by Phillip Keveren

Party Cat
Conductor's Score & Optional Accompaniment

Performance Configurations

Two Pianos

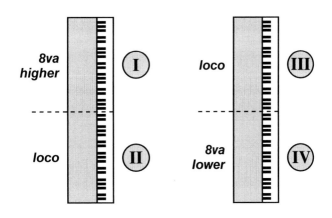

OR

Four Keyboards
(with suggested instrumentation)

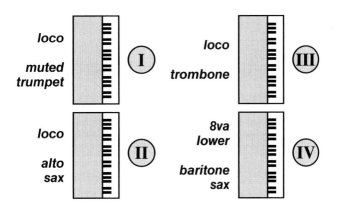

Party Cat

Written and arranged
by Phillip Keveren

Rockin' (♩ = 110)

Lies a - round and sleeps all day, rocks the night a - way!

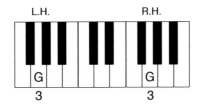

Night Shadows

Part I

Barbara Kreader
Arranged by Phillip Keveren

Quietly ($\quarternote$ = 82)

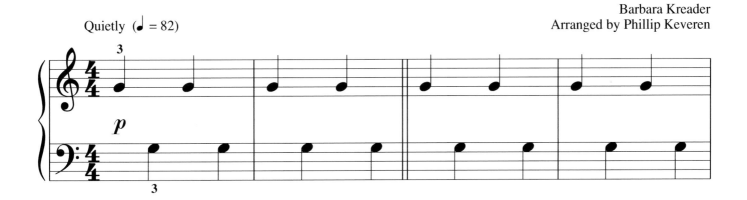

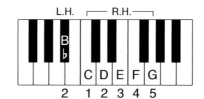

Party Cat

Part I

Written and arranged
by Phillip Keveren

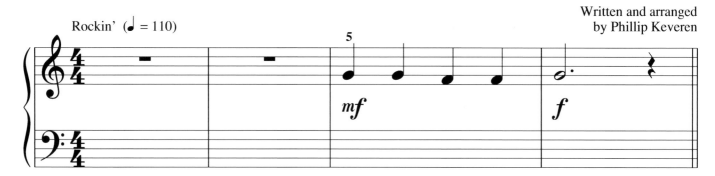

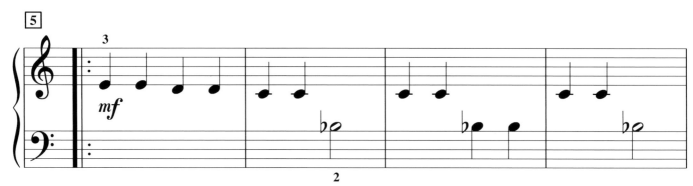

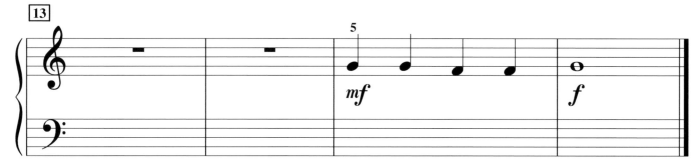

If you are:
- sharing the keyboard with *Part I*, **play as written**.
- seated at your own keyboard, **play as written**.

Suggested instrumentation: **piano**

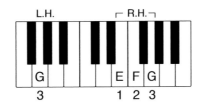

Night Shadows

Part II

Barbara Kreader
Arranged by Phillip Keveren

Quietly (♩ = 82)

11

If you are:
- sharing the keyboard with *Part I*, **play as written**.
- seated at your own keyboard, **play as written**.

Suggested instrumentation:
alto sax

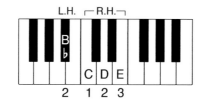

Party Cat

Part II

Written and arranged
by Phillip Keveren

Rockin' (♩ = 110)

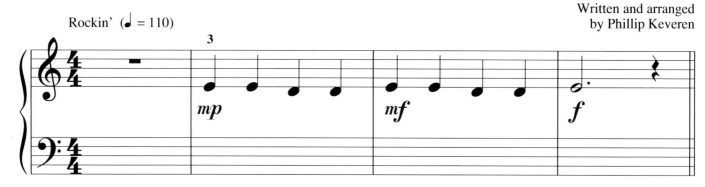

mp   mf   f

Rock 'n' roll is where it's at for my fam-'ly's par-ty cat.

mf

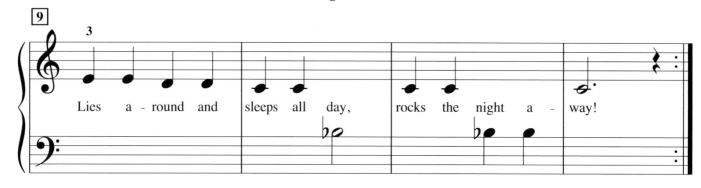

Lies a-round and sleeps all day, rocks the night a-way!

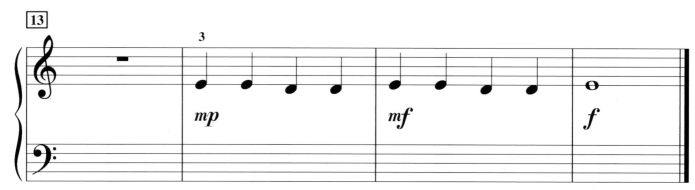

mp   mf   f

DO NOT PHOTOCOPY

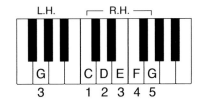

Night Shadows
Part III

Barbara Kreader
Arranged by Phillip Keveren

Quietly (♩ = 82)

If you are:
- sharing the keyboard with *Part IV*, **play as written**.
- seated at your own keyboard, **play as written**.

Suggested instrumentation:
trombone

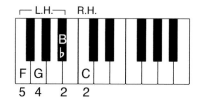

Party Cat
Part III

Written and arranged
by Phillip Keveren

Rockin' (♩ = 110)

© Hal Leonard

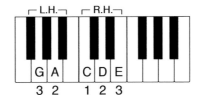

Night Shadows

Part IV

Barbara Kreader
Arranged by Phillip Keveren

Quietly (♩ = 82)

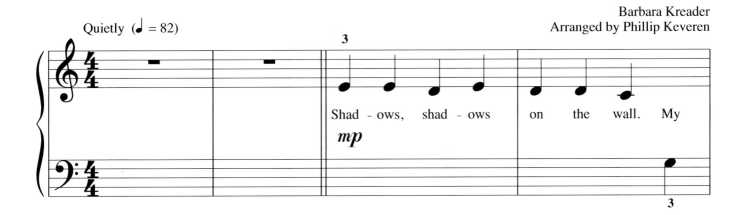

Shad - ows, shad - ows on the wall. My

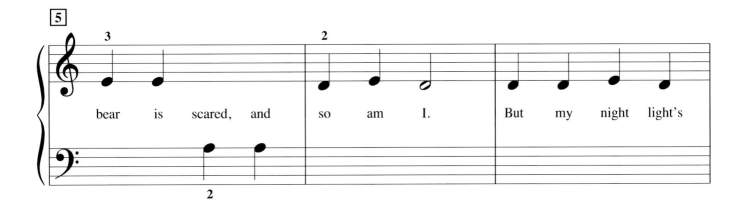

bear is scared, and so am I. But my night light's

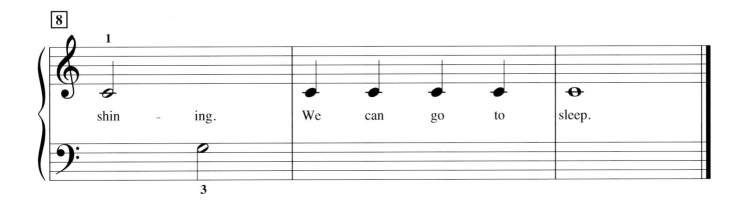

shin - ing. We can go to sleep.

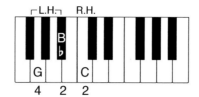

Party Cat

Part IV

Written and arranged
by Phillip Keveren

Trumpet Man
(Camptown Races)

Conductor's Score & Optional Accompaniment

Performance Configurations

Two Pianos

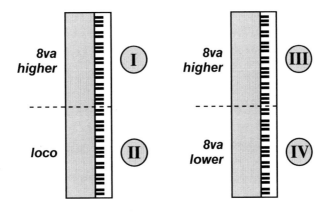

OR

Four Keyboards
(with suggested instrumentation)

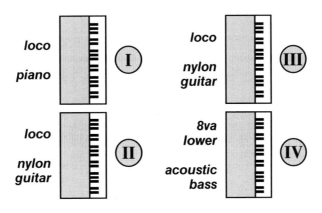

Trumpet Man

"Camptown Races"
Arranged by Phillip Keveren

Go For The Gold

Conductor's Score & Optional Accompaniment

Performance Configurations

Two Pianos

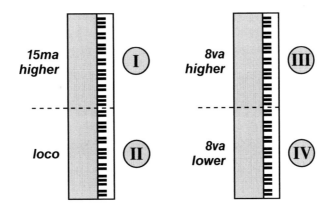

OR

Four Keyboards
(with suggested instrumentation)

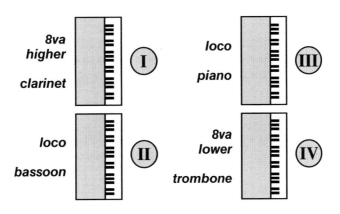

Go For The Gold

Written and arranged
by Phillip Keveren

Stately March ($\quad$ = 90)

If you are:
- sharing the keyboard with *Part II*, **play one octave higher**.
- seated at your own keyboard, **play as written**.

Suggested instrumentation:
piano

Trumpet Man

Part I

"Camptown Races"
Arranged by Phillip Keveren

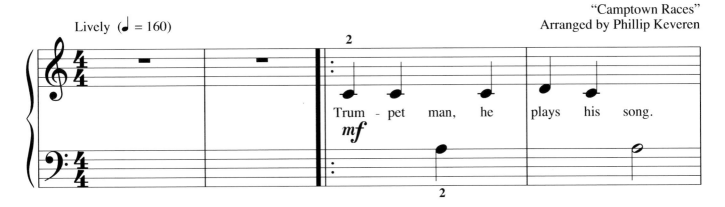

Lively (♩ = 160)

Trum - pet man, he   plays   his   song.

mf

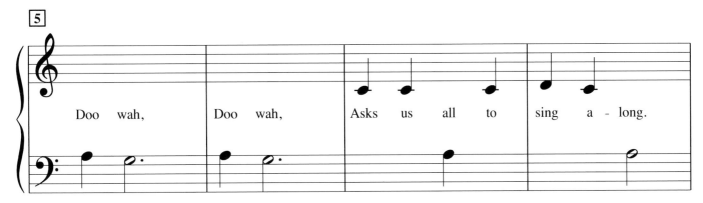

Doo   wah,   Doo   wah,   Asks   us   all   to   sing   a - long.

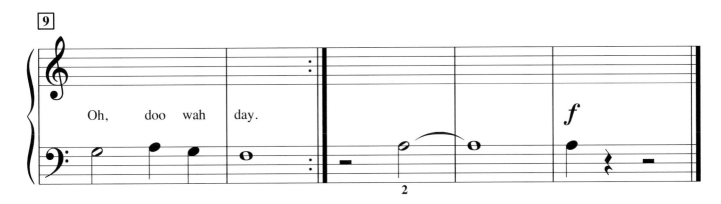

Oh,   doo   wah   day.

f

If you are:
- sharing the keyboard with *Part II*, **play two octaves higher**.
- seated at your own keyboard, **play one octave higher**.

Suggested instrumentation:
clarinet

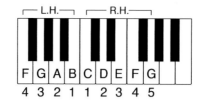

Go For The Gold

Part I

Written and arranged
by Phillip Keveren

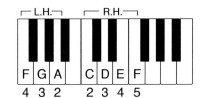

Trumpet Man

Part II

"Camptown Races"
Arranged by Phillip Keveren

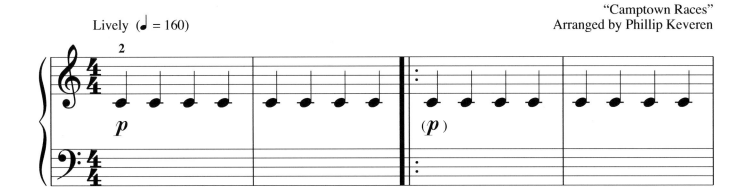

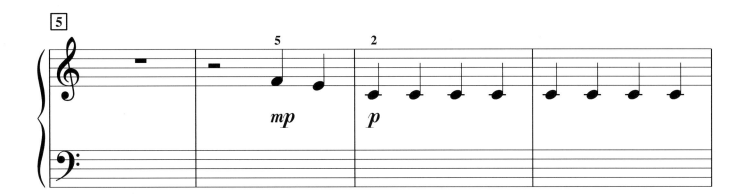

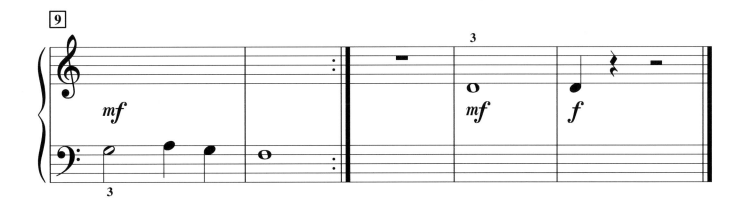

© Hal Leonard

If you are:
• sharing the keyboard with *Part I*,
  play as written.
• seated at your own keyboard,
  play as written.

Suggested instrumentation:
bassoon

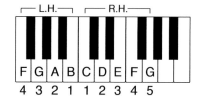

Go For The Gold

Part II

Written and arranged
by Phillip Keveren

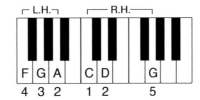

Trumpet Man
Part III

"Camptown Races"
Arranged by Phillip Keveren

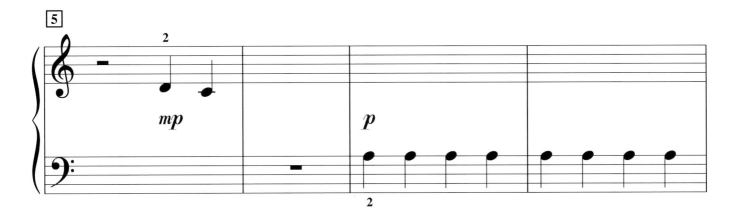

© Hal Leonard

If you are:
- sharing the keyboard with *Part IV*, **play one octave higher**.
- seated at your own keyboard, **play as written**.

Suggested instrumentation: **piano**

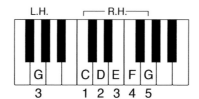

Go For The Gold

Part III

Written and arranged
by Phillip Keveren

Stately March (♩ = 90)

If you are:
- sharing the keyboard with *Part III*,
  play one octave lower.
- seated at your own keyboard,
  play one octave lower.

Suggested instrumentation:
acoustic bass

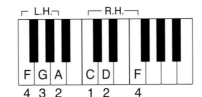

Trumpet Man

Part IV

"Camptown Races"
Arranged by Phillip Keveren

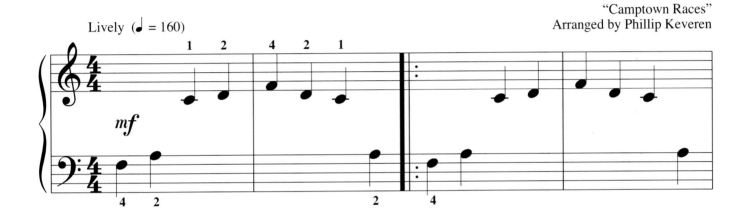

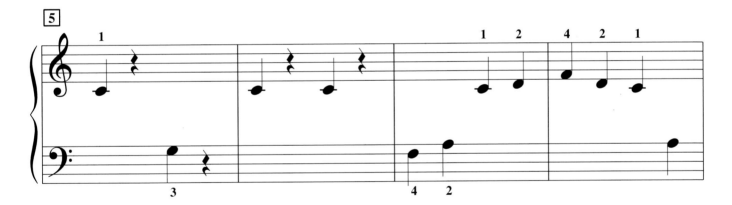

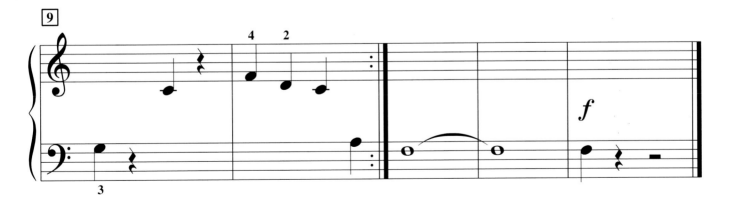

If you are:
- sharing the keyboard with *Part III*, **play one octave lower.**
- seated at your own keyboard, **play one octave lower.**

Suggested instrumentation: **trombone**

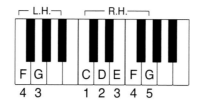

Go For The Gold

Part IV

Written and arranged
by Phillip Keveren

Stately March (♩ = 90)

© Hal Leonard